Rourke
Educational Media
rourkeeducationalmedia.com

A Division of
Carson
Dellosa
Education

OFF-ROAD
VEHICLES

JEEPS

GARY SPROTT

BEFORE AND DURING READING ACTIVITIES

Before Reading: *Building Background Knowledge and Vocabulary*

Building background knowledge can help children process new information and build upon what they already know. Before reading a book, it is important to tap into what children already know about the topic. This will help them develop their vocabulary and increase their reading comprehension.

Questions and Activities to Build Background Knowledge:

1. Look at the front cover of the book and read the title. What do you think this book will be about?
2. What do you already know about this topic?
3. Take a book walk and skim the pages. Look at the table of contents, photographs, captions, and bold words. Did these text features give you any information or predictions about what you will read in this book?

Vocabulary: *Vocabulary Is Key to Reading Comprehension*

Use the following directions to prompt a conversation about each word.

- Read the vocabulary words.
- What comes to mind when you see each word?
- What do you think each word means?

Vocabulary Words:
- *assemble*
- *grueling*
- *combat*
- *traction*
- *enthusiastic*
- *versatile*

During Reading: *Reading for Meaning and Understanding*

To achieve deep comprehension of a book, children are encouraged to use close reading strategies. During reading, it is important to have children stop and make connections. These connections result in deeper analysis and understanding of a book.

 Close Reading a Text

During reading, have children stop and talk about the following:

- Any confusing parts
- Any unknown words
- Text to text, text to self, text to world connections
- The main idea in each chapter or heading

Encourage children to use context clues to determine the meaning of any unknown words. These strategies will help children learn to analyze the text more thoroughly as they read.

When you are finished reading this book, turn to the next-to-last page for **After Reading Questions** and an **Activity**.

TABLE OF CONTENTS

MUD-SLINGING MARVELS

Ready to splash through streams, scramble across rocks, and kick up some dirt? Buckle up for a thrilling ride in the rugged Wrangler or the classy Cherokee. The Jeep brand's legendary off-road vehicles have been exploring new trails for nearly 80 years!

What's in a Name?

The word *jeep* may have come from the military term *GP*, for *General Purpose*. Later, Jeep became the brand name for a line of off-road vehicles.

Four-wheel drive technology gives Jeep automobiles tremendous **traction**. With all four tires gripping the ground, these agile autos can handle the trickiest terrain! Fallen logs blocking the path? No problem. Extra clearance under the chassis lets the vehicle clamber over obstacles.

traction (TRAK-shuhn): the gripping force that keeps a moving object from slipping on a surface

Global Power

The Jeep brand is owned by Fiat Chrysler Automobiles. About two million Jeeps were sold worldwide in 2018!

The Jeep Wrangler's famous design allows owners to change several features. Want to feel the sun and wind on your face in the great outdoors? Doors and windows are removable. The windshield folds down, and soft or hard tops can be lowered or simply taken off.

Holy Toledo!

The Jeep Wrangler is built in Toledo, Ohio. More than 5,000 people—and hundreds of robots—**assemble** vehicles at the massive complex. It's so big that more than 50 soccer fields could fit inside!

assemble (uh-SEM-buhl): to put all the parts of something together

9

It takes both brain and brawn to handle the harshest conditions. Jeeps have mighty muscle under the hood. With a V6 engine that delivers up to 285 horsepower, the Wrangler has enough power to tow up to 3,500 pounds (1,588 kilograms). That's as heavy as a couple of Clydesdale horses!

The Jeep Cherokee has been a trendsetter among sport utility vehicles (SUVs) since it hit the market in 1984. It was the first-ever vehicle with part-time and full-time four-wheel drive options. The Cherokee combines comfort and style with off-road capabilities.

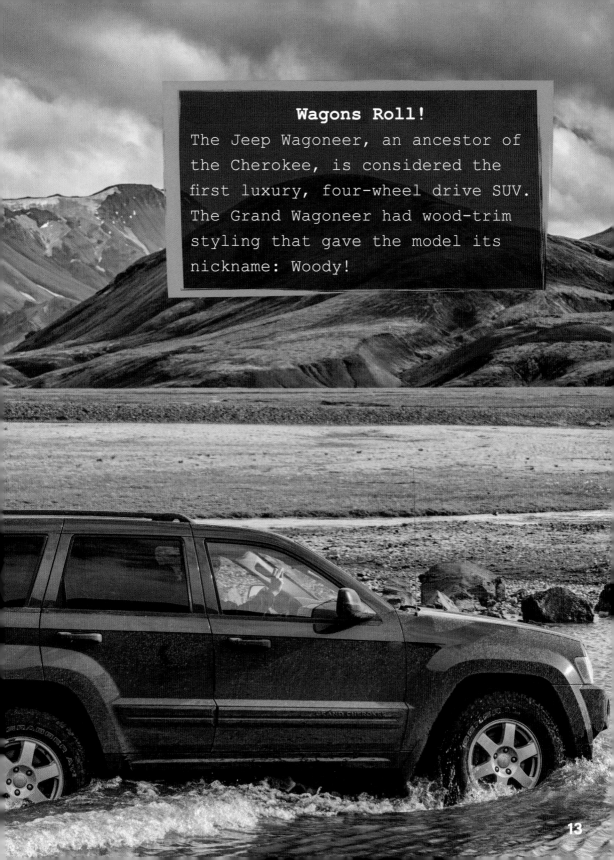

Wagons Roll!

The Jeep Wagoneer, an ancestor of the Cherokee, is considered the first luxury, four-wheel drive SUV. The Grand Wagoneer had wood-trim styling that gave the model its nickname: Woody!

WHEELED WARRIORS

Jeeps were born during the 1940s. The United States Army needed a **versatile** vehicle for soldiers fighting in World War II. The first jeeps, known as Willys, were lightweight and could be transported to battlefields by airplanes and gliders.

versatile (VUR-suh-tuhl): able to be used in many ways

Are Jeeps Cheap?

Willys jeeps cost about 738 dollars each. A new Jeep Wrangler will cost you about 28,000 dollars.

Jeeps were wartime wonders. They were used for patrolling, snow plowing, towing, and firefighting. They served as ambulances or got equipped with machine guns for **combat**. Jeeps could even be fitted with special wheels to run on railroad tracks!

combat (KAHM-bat): fighting between people or armies

This Willy jeep was photographed at the Desert Training Center in Indio, California, in 1942.

The jeep legend grew quickly. One news reporter described the vehicle as "faithful as a dog, strong as a mule, and agile as a goat." One jeep known as "Old Faithful" was hit by gunfire during fighting on a Pacific Ocean island. It was awarded an honorary Purple Heart medal for being wounded in action!

Don't Toy with Jeeps!
Jeeps aren't just popular with real-life heroes. The G.I. Joe action figure relies on his trusty jeep when it's time to battle bad guys!

TOUGH TRAILBLAZERS

After helping America and its allies win World War II, jeeps were used to help feed America. The vehicles were redesigned so millions of farmers could replace horses with horsepower! The peacetime jeep was a workhorse that could haul heavy loads on the farm and in the fields.

Jeeps go through **grueling** tests to make sure they are ready to master the toughest tasks. Engineers and test drivers expose new vehicles to frozen wilderness, overflowing creeks, and desert canyons. One of the biggest challenges is the 22-mile (35-kilometer) Rubicon Trail in California's Sierra Nevada Mountains.

grueling (GROO-uh-ling): very demanding and tiring

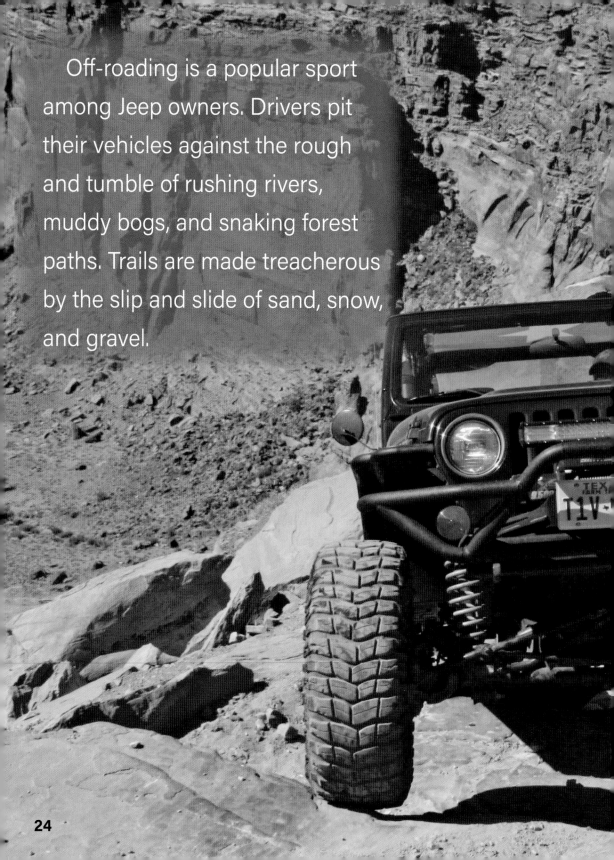

Off-roading is a popular sport among Jeep owners. Drivers pit their vehicles against the rough and tumble of rushing rivers, muddy bogs, and snaking forest paths. Trails are made treacherous by the slip and slide of sand, snow, and gravel.

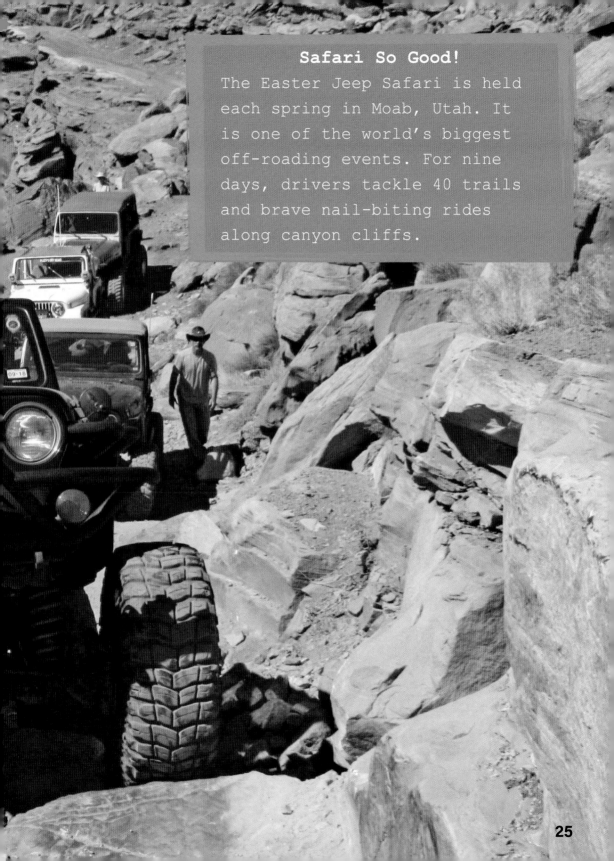

Safari So Good!

The Easter Jeep Safari is held each spring in Moab, Utah. It is one of the world's biggest off-roading events. For nine days, drivers tackle 40 trails and brave nail-biting rides along canyon cliffs.

Enthusiastic off-roaders can earn Jeep's Badge of Honor. Drivers download an app that gives the location and difficulty of trails across the United States. As they complete trails such as Cliff Hanger, Crawl Daddy, and Black Bear Pass, drivers get badges to display on their vehicles.

enthusiastic (en-thoo-zee-AS-tik): having feelings of excitement and great interest

Jeeps are vital in emergencies because of their awesome ability to go off the beaten track. First responders use four-wheel drive vehicles to deliver food, water, and medical supplies during hurricanes and other natural disasters. They can also transport citizens to safety from dangerous areas.

Revved Up for Rescues!

Many Jeep owners belong to search-and-rescue groups. These on-call volunteers drive into secluded areas to help find missing or stranded people. They are trained to provide first aid and other assistance.

Memory Game

Look at the pictures. What do you remember reading on the pages where each image appeared?

Index

After Reading Questions

1. How many Jeeps were sold worldwide in 2018?

2. Where is the Jeep Wrangler built?

3. Why was the Jeep Grand Wagoneer nicknamed "Woody"?

4. Where is the Easter Jeep Safari held each year?

5. What military honor did the jeep known as "Old Faithful" receive?

Activity

In your backyard or at a local park, use natural items you find to create a miniature off-road trail. Imagine pebbles or stones are boulders or rocks. Turn twigs and branches into fallen logs. How would your jeep get past these obstacles?

About the Author

Gary Sprott is a writer in Tampa, Florida. He has owned two Jeep Wranglers. He loved driving around with the top down—except during the Sunshine State's summer thunderstorms!

www.rourkeeducationalmedia.com

PHOTO CREDITS: Cover, title page, 24-25: ©Ogletree/Shutterstock; p.5, 30: ©Sunshine Seeds/Shutterstock; p.7: ©Nathanial Adams; p.9, 30: ©MousePotato; p.10-11: ©Viktoriia1208, Winged Horse Productions (horses); p.13: ©Sjoerd van der Wal; p.15: ©the_guitar_mann, ©Route55 (money); p.16-17, 21, 30: Library of Congress; p.19, 30: ©Michal Rybski; p.18: ©Brendan Hunter (toy jeep), Gregory_DUBOS (toy soldier); p.22: ©Paul Vaschenkov; p.26: ©PhoThoughts; p.27, 30: ©Pan_Photo/Shutterstock; p.29, 30: © Cheryle Myers | Dreamstime.com

Edited by: Kim Thompson
Cover and interior design by: Rhea Magaro-Wallace

Library of Congress PCN Data

Jeeps / Gary Sprott
(Off-Road Vehicles)
ISBN 978-1-73161-457-5 (hard cover)
ISBN 978-1-73161-258-8 (soft cover)
ISBN 978-1-73161-562-6 (e-Book)
ISBN 978-1-73161-667-8 (ePub)
Library of Congress Control Number: 2019932358

Rourke Educational Media
Printed in the United States of America,
North Mankato, Minnesota

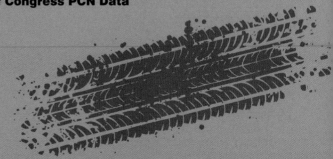